# Crystal Grids for Personal Protection

## By

## S. D. Anderson, Ph.D., RMT

©2018 by Sharon D. Anderson, PhD, RMT



Cape Cod Publishing

Cape Cod, MA 02632

ISBN-13: 978-1724362926

ISBN-10:1724362925

This book is dedicated to my Angels and Guides.

They always help me find the correct crystal for whatever condition we are dealing with. Their insights are uncanny!

*"Keep your energy strong and no harm can befall you."*

*-Ancient Chinese Proverb*

# Contents

Acknowledgments

I would be lost without Judy Hall's fabulous books on crystals:

*The Crystal Bible, 101 Power Crystals, Crystal Prescriptions, Crystal Healing,* and *more.*

*Plato's Platonic Solids and Sacred Geometry*

Kitty Elder who kindled my interest in grids

David Hatcher-Childress and his work: *Anti-Gravity and the World Grid.*

Becker-Hagens: *Pythagorean Cosmic Morphology*

And to my Unseens and Guides who gave remarkable input.

For these sources, I give grateful thanks…

Other Crystal Books by S. D. Anderson, Ph.D. available on Amazon.com

*Creating Crystal Grids for Beginners*

A step by step guide to creating your grids.

https://www.amazon.com/Creating-Crystal-Grids-Sharon-Anderson-ebook/dp/B00BPCWKI2/

*Sacred Grids*

A guide to using the Sacred Geometry connection in grids

https://www.amazon.com/Sacred-Grids-Creating-Crystal-Geometry-ebook/dp/B00UDMZN4S/

*Crystal Grids: Activating the 12 Strands of DNA*

An advanced book on grids

https://www.amazon.com/Crystal-Grids-Activating-Strands-DNA-ebook/dp/B0182I7L1M/

# Introduction

Amazing how manuscripts manifest. I am always in awe when some thought comes to life on my computer screen, and morphs into a book.

The concept for this book has been hovering on my screen for several months, and in my thoughts for a little longer. I knew I would write it eventually--- and true to form, my unseens placed me in an environment of such toxicity, that I was forced to do something about it.

As a writer of a lot of books over a lot of years, I know that you write and teach about what you have to learn, OR you write from experience. (very funny, guys!)

Over the years, I have always protected myself and my family and friends; a ritual I do each morning, nevertheless, times have changed and so have the energies around us. What worked before, didn't seem to be working now. What was I doing or not doing? More importantly, what should I be doing?

When times are occasionally challenging, or a certain condition arises, (either physical, emotional, or environmental) I revert back to my crystals, using them to protect, transmute, heal, or harmonize the situation. My experience with them has always been successful. They are my go-to, my 'blue blankie', and I believe in their amazing qualities and their 'special' healing powers. How crystals and grids work, and why we need them especially now will be explained, So, keep reading. No, this is not Sci-Fi, although you may think so at first. It is a different way to look at the earth and the ground you are standing on.

Happy Gridding

Sharon

Cape Cod

August 2018

I have divided the book into five parts:

1. Why You Need Protection

2. All about your Grids

3. Protecting your Person

4. Protecting your Home

5. Protecting your Workplace

# Part One - Why You Need Protection

Here is the dictionary meaning of the noun:

**protection**

the action of protecting someone or something, or the state of being protected. To be kept safe.

A few questions to help you understand why you may need protection, or why you need to be kept safe.

Let's work with personal boundaries first:

Personal Boundaries

*Am I able to say no?*

*Do people come to me with their troubles?*

*Do I feel overwhelmed by people's emotions or thoughts?*

*Can I take time for myself without feeling guilty?*

Did any of those resonate? You may not think you are giving your energy away, but if you answered yes to one of those questions, you need to have some measure of protection. These are some of the qualities of an EMPATH. An Empath is someone who takes on other people's troubles, emotions, or drama.

Here are a few more questions to answer……

*Do you read or watch programs about sensational psychic activity?*

*Are you meddling or dabbling in psychic things without being trained?*

*Do you believe you are psychic or have a sixth sense?*

*Do you meditate?*

*Do you worry excessively about what is going on in the world?*

<u>*How are your answers so far?*</u>

*Have you got your head in the clouds?*

*Are you grounded and in your body?*

*Do you use recreational drugs?*

*Do you give energy to other people?*

*Does using a computer make you tired?*

*Do certain people or places leave you feeling drained?*

(Shopping Malls will do this.)

*Do you cry easily?*

*Do you feel sad if a friend is depressed or unhappy?*

*Do you feel on edge if a friend is angry?*

*Are you accident-prone?*

*Have small things gone wrong recently*

*Do you lose things?*

*Do you have nightmares and insomnia?*

*Do you sleep through the night?*

*Are you anxious, nervous, on edge?*

*Are you afraid to relax?*

*Are you perpetually tired, listless, hopeless?*

*Have you ever felt invaded, somehow not yourself?*

*Were you born under the zodiac sign of*

*Cancer, Scorpio, or Pisces?*

*Have you ever seen a ghost or felt bad vibes?*

*Do certain people give you chills?*

<u>If you can answer yes to some of those questions, you might want to keep reading.</u>

*Source:* Most of these questions and ideas come from *Crystals for Psychic Self-Protection* by Judy Hall (2014) some from personal experience.

# Some Common Energy Drains You Might Not Have Thought Existed

**Psychic attack:** concentrated and conscious malevolent thought and intent directed towards someone to bring about harm. Sometimes this is not consciously intended but done unconsciously as the person thinks negative thoughts about another person or discusses this person with someone else.

**Psychic mugging:** being hit by a blast of negative energy., either from the environment or another person.

**Sick Building Syndrome:** the set of symptoms, including headaches, dizziness, nausea, chest problems, and general fatigue, associated with buildings with actual air pollution or inadequate ventilation, or negative environmental energies.

**Geo-pathic stress:** stress created by electromagnetic radiation, ley lines, underground water, etc.

It's also present in 'sick building syndrome'. Injurious to health, it can affect the immune system as well as the body's innate psychic protection and may attract "ghosts" or hold impressions of previous events.

**Electromagnetic stress:** disharmony caused by the subtle emanations of electrical, microwave, computer, phone and radio frequencies, and power lines.

Don't stress out over these, you just need to know they exist, that they are all around you.

Keep reading:

# What Is Psychic Self-Protection?

**Psychic self-protection is** creating a safe space around your body, and within yourself, by screening out unwanted thoughts, feelings, and energies from other people and the environment. It's about preventing energy loss to other people or the environment.

It's also about having positive emotions and constructive thoughts that create a benevolent world. It isn't really about doing, it's all about creating through your own thoughts.

Psychic Self Protection creates a tranquil space in which others cannot disturb you or your balance, either deliberately or by what they think or feel.

**Protecting Your Aura:** Your energy field or the subtle bio magnetic sheath that surrounds your physical body is the first line of defense and needs constant protection and strengthening.

A quick and easy way to protect yourself if you are sitting with a needy person, a troubled friend or at someone at work that you feel uncomfortable with, cross your arms over your solar plexus and cross your legs at the ankles to create an energy circuit that cannot be breached.

A time honored and reliable means of protecting yourself is by wearing a crystal or keeping one in your pocket.

Although, if you don't ask the Crystal to work with you and you forget to keep it energetically clean afterwards it can end up doing the opposite of what you intended it to do, so do remember to clean all your crystals regularly.

Most of these questions and ideas come from *Crystals for Psychic Self-Protection* by Judy Hall (2014)

**The Three Breaths.**

Whenever you feel the need to ground yourself or feel calm and quiet, three breaths are all you need to do the trick.

Find a quiet spot. If you need to excuse yourself and hide in the rest room do it. Or, just sit in your parked vehicle. Get someplace where you will not be disturbed for at least 5 minutes and try this exercise.

Sit quietly, close your eyes and take one deep breath and release it. Don't think about anything. Just focus on your breath and your breathing. Feel your body starting to relax a little bit. You can take normal breaths between the three big breaths.

Take another deep breath, this time breathe in through your nose and out through your mouth releasing any tension. Feel your shoulders relax. Again, focus on your breathing.

Now, take your third deep breath, consciously let it out quietly, focusing on that breath, making it as long as you can, releasing any inner tension.

When you feel sufficiently calm, open your eyes and know you're ready to face whatever situation it was that was making you tense or nervous.

Hold one of your crystals as you do this exercise. The simple act of holding it in your hand will remind yourself to look at the situation differently.

# Part Two - All About Your Grids

A note about your crystals before we begin……

## Cleansing your crystals...

Hold them under running water for a few minutes and place them in the sun for a few hours.  If there is no sun, visualize brilliant white light radiating down onto them.

It is important to keep them cleansed after each use. If you keep them in a box or a bag, a clear quartz or an orange carnelian will automatically keep them clear.

## Activating your crystals...

Hold them in your hands, close your eyes and concentrate on them.

See them surrounded with brilliant white light.

Ask that they be attuned to your unique

frequency, that they be activated to act as healers at any level that you may need now or in the future.

Ask that they be blessed with the highest energies in the universe and dedicated to your self-healing and that of the environment around you.

Source: Crystal Healing by Judy Hall

Also, a free booklet on "the Care and Feeding of your Crystals" on my website

www.audacious-publisher.com

# Descriptions Of The Crystals We Use In This Book

## Labradorite.

The number one protection Crystal, Labradorite creates an interface around you that filters out energies that are not to your benefit and enhances your spiritual connection. It allows you to be aware of other people's feelings and energies without being overwhelmed by them. Enhancing your psychic abilities, it aligns the physical and subtle bodies and strengthens the aura.

## Smokey quartz

One of the major stones for drawing off or blocking negative energy, Smokey Quartz is an excellent antidote to stress or worry. It fortifies your resolve and support you in letting go of any patterns you no longer need. It also grounds you in your body and assist you in accepting physical incarnation.

## Amazonite

An excellent protection against geo-pathic and electromagnetic emanations of all kinds. Amazonite has a strong filtering action on the physical and mental levels. A soothing stone for emotional or physical trauma, it alleviates worry and assists in seeing both points of view.

## Green Aventurine

Green Aventurine is an excellent stone for preventing energy loss to energy pirates or to electromagnetic stress.

A stone of prosperity that opens and calms the heart, it's a useful gridding stone against environmental pollution.

It assists you to see and assess alternatives and possibilities and promotes emotional recovery.

## Obsidian-Black-

Linked with inner growth, positive change, fulfillment, introspection, practicality, stability, manifestation, and psychic development. Exposes our rationalizations and illusions. Obsidian is molten lava that cooled so quickly it had no time to crystallize. Protective, it repels negativity and disperses unloving thoughts. Obsidians greatest gift is insight into the cause of dis-ease.

## Fluorite-

Associated with consciousness, aura cleansing, truth and protection. All fluorite offers psychic protection and healing. Helps dissolve blocks, fixed ideas and small thinking. Stimulates regeneration of skin, mucous membranes, ulcers. Fortifies bones and teeth, decreases adhesions and helps with posture. Improves stiffness and joint problems (arthritis), makes us physically mobile. Place in your environment for a sense of order or can be carried or laid directly on body.

## Sodalite-

Unites logic w/intuition, clears electromagnetic pollution, brings harmony to group work, encourages rational thought, objectivity, truth, intuitive perception. Calms panic attacks, emotional balance, enhances self-esteem and self-acceptance. Balances the metabolism, calcium deficiencies, cleanses lymphatic system and organs. Combats radiation damage and insomnia. Cools fevers and lowers blood pressure. Place as appropriate or wear for long periods of time.

**Iron Pyrite—**

a yellow metallic mineral sometimes called 'fool's gold'. Augments intelligence, mental stability, logic, analysis, creativity, channeling abilities, memory, optimism, practicality and willpower. Blocks out negative energy and pollutants including infectious disease. Treats bones and stimulates cellular formation, repairs DNA damage and aligns the meridians, neutralizes ingested toxins, beneficial for the lungs, alleviating asthma and bronchitis. Wear or carry on person. Peru

## Clear Quartz -

The most powerful healing and energy amplifier on the planet. It absorbs, stores, releases and regulates energy and is excellent for unblocking it.  Works at a vibrational level attuned to the specific energy requirements of the person holding it.  Master healer, it can be used for any condition, stimulates immune systems, and brings the body back into balance. Brazil.

## Amethyst

a natural tranquilizer, amethyst distresses and protects you on all levels and provides emotional balance. It is useful for blocking geo-pathic stress and negative or noxious energies. Sitting quietly holding it will calm your mind and allow you to access the deeper parts of yourself to gain insight, and find new motivation.

## Quartz

the most prevalent Crystal on the planet, Quartz is excellent for amplifying, unblocking and generating energy. It cleanses and heals the body and other crystals, storing information and heightening perception in addition to forming a protective barrier that negative energies cannot cross. All the different forms of Quartz provide excellent psychic protection and most enhance your ability to raise your awareness and open your higher chakras.

## Tektite

Of extraterrestrial origin. Enhances communication with other worlds, encourages spiritual growth as it forms a link between creative energy and matter. Balances energy flow and chakras. enhances telepathy and clairvoyance. Helps release undesirable experiences. Placed on third eye, it opens communication with other dimensions. Strengthens the biomagnetic sheath around the body.

**Crystal Points–** Quartz crystals usually have 6 facets which equate to the 6 chakras from the base to the third eye and the termination point representing the crown and its link to the infinite. A single point is usually used in healing. Pointed away from the body it draws energy off. Pointed inward, it channels energy into the body. Quartz crystals that are totally clear are symbols of cosmic harmony. Keeping one with you will align your energy to the spiritual realm.

**Apophyllite**—enables and strengthens conscious intended connection with the spiritual world. It is an energy stimulator that brings high crystal energy to mystical and other endeavors. When placed on the third eye chakra, it enhances clairvoyance and mystical vision, particularly when using the natural pyramid form. This can help one see the truth on many planes in a way that facilitates bringing this truth to the Earth plane for use in spiritual growth and connection. Apophyllite is also used to assist in contacting and working with Guardian Angels, Spirit Guides, and manifestations of the Higher Self.

# Choosing Your Crystals

There are several tried and true ways to choose a crystal.

1.     **The visual approach** – you choose a crystal that looks beautiful or is visually attractive. Your eye is instinctively drawn to it and you cannot 'see' any other.

2.     **The Intuitive approach** – you close your eyes and allow your intuition to choose your crystal for you as you gently run your hand over the selection of crystals. The one that 'sticks to' your hand is the one you need to take home.

3.      **The 'gifted' approach** – you are the recipient of a certain crystal that is given to you.


4.      **The 'brain' approach** – you need a crystal for a certain purpose and you seek that crystal out as the one that was meant to do the task at hand. Usually you would look up in a directory or listing for that particular condition, note the various crystals with those exact properties, and make your selection from there.

# Opening The Hand Chakra

Before choosing a crystal by any method, it is best to open the hand chakra.

In the center of each palm there is an energy point. In Chinese Medicine and Qigong this point is called the La Gong point. In Reiki, which is a Japanese Healing Technique, the energy comes into the crown, travels down into the heart and out through the palms. (The La Gong Point.) This is a very powerful energy point.

This point is also very sensitive to the touch and naturally sensitive to energies. It is a good idea to open this point when you are going to do any work with crystals, especially if you are choosing a crystal or asking it to work with you.

To open this chakra, take several deep breaths to center yourself, and ask for guidance from any of your Higher Beings or your Higher Self. When you are ready, gently rub the center of your palm in a circular motion, usually clockwise, but choose whatever direction is most comfortable for you. When you feel the chakra is warm and 'tingly' . . .

Reiki students can just do a symbol over the spot.

Now you are ready to work with your crystals.

The grids shown in this book are composed of several crystals or stones in a certain alignment. You get to choose which alignment you want to use as you plan your grid. In all the grids, we use either polished or raw stones. You also get to choose which stones you want or are appropriate.

The stones or crystals used in this book are:

Clear Quartz

Smokey Quartz

Apophyllite

Amethyst

Crystal Points

Amazonite

Labradorite

Fluorite

Sodalite,

Green Aventurine,

Iron Pyrite,

Tektite

Don't worry if you don't have all these stones, you can always substitute clear crystals or any other crystal you may have that will work as effectively.

# What are grids and what do we use them for?

Grids are energetic transmitters. They are like two-way radios that create an energetic field that will either bring energy down or send it out. When we create a grid, we are either calling in energy to be released into the environment for some purpose or intent or sending the energy out into the atmosphere for transmutation or for distant spiritual healing.

The most common configurations for grids are in geometric shapes; triangles, squares, stars, circles, etc.

When we create our grids, we are calling upon the strength and the energetic qualities of these eternal geometric shapes to work in conjunction with these grids. We are asking for their assistance. It is my belief that the grids we create work in harmony with the sacred geometry shapes.

The 5 Platonic Solids are ideal, primal models of crystal patterns that occur throughout the world of minerals in countless variations. These are the only five regular polyhedrons, that is, the only five solids made from the same equilateral, equiangular polygons. Pure quartz crystal has been cut from these primal shapes to be used in meditation, healing, and manifestation.

When we create our grids, we are calling upon the strength and the energetic qualities of these eternal geometric shapes to work in conjunction with these grids. We are asking for their assistance.

It is my belief that that the grids that we create work in harmony with these sacred geometry shapes.

These geometric symbols are visual instruments that can help bring our vibrations into harmony with the rhythms of nature. The same refined, regenerative technology that nature has evolved can be used in ways to help organize our own thought patterns…

# The Grids and their Sacred Geometry Connection:

The Triangle or THREE STONE GRID is a basic configuration and resonates to the Tetrahedron which represents Creation and Manifestation and Manifestation Form. It resonates with the Solar Plexus Chakra; Color is Red, Element is Fire. You will see this shape again as it works with the Star of David Grid or the Six- pointed grid.

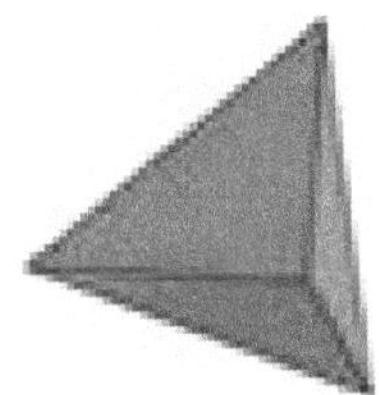

I believe that a FOUR STONE GRID is a foundation grid and resonates with the sacred geometric shape of the Hexahedron or (Cube) - Grounding, Creation- Grounding Form.  Base Chakra, Color is Green, Element is Earth.

Next, we have the FIVE STONE GRID or the star grid which resonates to the dodecahedron. The Dodecahedron – Representing: the Twelve Faces of the Divine within - Ascension and Mystery. School Forms, Spirit Chakras, Color is Gold, Element is Ether.

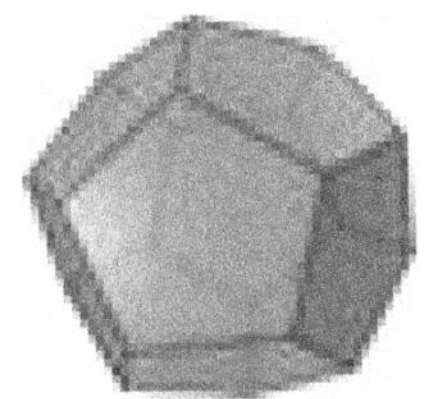

Next are the SIX STONE GRIDS which resonate with the Merkabah or the six-pointed star or the Tetrahedron. Tetrahedron –represents Creation and Manifestation - Manifestation Form. Resonates with the Solar Plexus Chakra; Color is Red, Element is Fire.

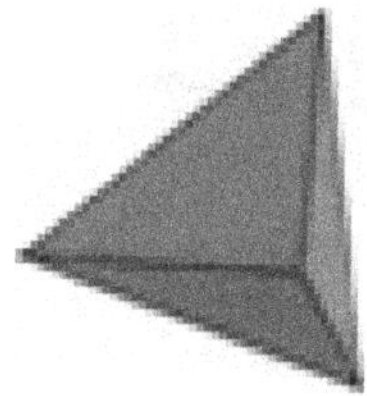

The EIGHT STONE GRID resonates with the octahedron. The Octahedron – represents the Eight Paths to Enlightenment - Integrative Form; resonates with the Heart Chakra, Color is Yellow, Element is Air.

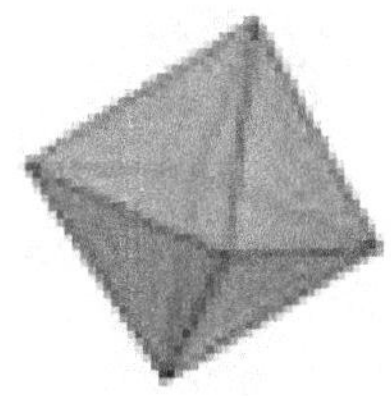

Now, the TWELVE STONE GRID resonates with the icosahedron: Icosahedrons – represent Conscious Prayer and Transformation Form; Navel Chakra, Color is Blue, Element is Water. (20 faces)

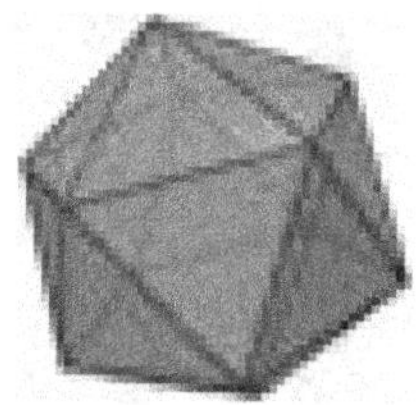

For the purposes of this book, we recommend using **the four stone** grid or hexahedron (this shape is used to grid in a room or a house or a building).

**The five stone grid or dodecahedron** (five-pointed star) which will have many uses. This shape is easily recreated visually or drawn in the air. Before you enter your vehicle to drive, trace a star or a dodecahedron above it for protection. Use this process any time you are somewhere, and you feel uncomfortable. See this star or pentagram over your head beaming down protection. I am certain our Forefathers knew the value of the 'star' when it was used to represent each state in the Union.

**The six stone grid** or the most common grid, relates to the Star of David (two intertwined triangles bringing balance as the top triangle brings energy down and the base triangle brings energy up)

To use the rest of the grid configurations, I recommend my other books, *Creating Crystal Grids for Beginners, and Sacred Grids*

.

# Choosing Your Center Stone:

You can choose wonderful crystals for your grid and they will carry out your intent, but the force, the single force that ties it all together is the central crystal or stone.  That is the one that gathers the energy from each stone and propels it up and out into the atmosphere, into the universe to harness the energy and set it into the pattern you chose when you selected the grid configuration you were going to use. Normally, this is done for us by our unseen beings surrounding us but sometimes it is a good idea to be mindful of what and where you want to focus these energies.

Consider, if you will, the following stones for the center of your grid for their high attunement and energetic qualities

<u>Clusters</u> tend to diffuse the energies and send them up and out in a gentle way

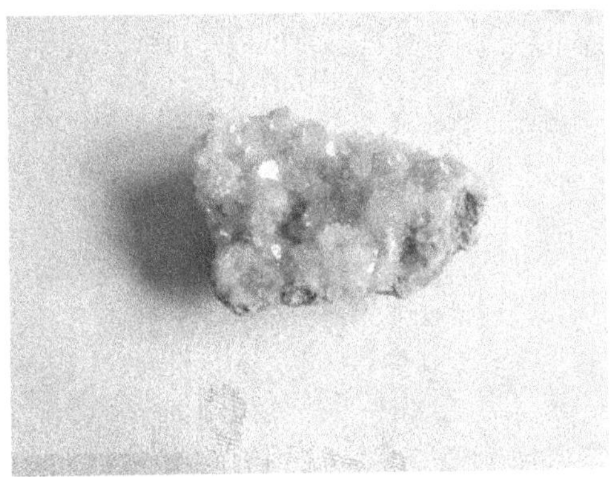

<u>This is a Celestite Cluster.</u>

**Celestite -** Madagascar - A stone of high vibrations, teacher for New Realms, it is imbued with Divine Energy. Stimulates clairvoyant communications, dream recall and out-of-body journeys. Heals the aura, brings balance and alignment, heals disorders of the eyes and ears, eliminates toxins, brings cellular order. A large piece placed in a room heightens the vibration. Direct sunlight will fade colors

<u>Pyramids</u> - Crystals cut in a pyramid shape is a good choice, because it gathers and sends upward the energies of your surrounding crystals.

Apophyllite are naturally pyramidal shaped and are excellent choices but any crystals either natural or cut in the pyramid shape are great energy propellants.

<u>Pointed</u> - Any crystal that has a peak can be used equally. I have used many different stones and crystals for the centers and they all work equally as well. The most important thing to remember is the **'intent'** behind it.

Now that you have determined which grid layout you wish to use (keep it simple to start with if you are new at this) and you have chosen the crystals you want to use, find a place where your grid will remain undisturbed for a few days and clear the area.

You can do this by literally cleaning the area (dusting, polishing, or vacuuming) and remove any peripheral objects that may interfere with the energy of the grid. Remove all clutter, magazines, newspapers, soiled laundry, etc.… and clean the space.

Now CLEAR the space from any unwanted energies that may interfere with your grid and its purpose.

You can use any number of things to do this; sage, incense, a lighted candle, a Tibetan

Bowl, etc.... and once this is done, you are ready to lay out your grid.

# Completing Your Preparation

## A CHECKLIST

Now that you have done all the prep work;

Chosen your stones,

Cleared the stones,

Dedicated or programmed your stones,

Chosen your center stone

Chosen your grid configuration

Chosen your location

You are ready to set up your grid.

# Activating Your Grid

Place the crystals in your chosen configuration allowing enough room for the center stone and put that in place.

Watch your alignment. If they flip and flop, you can set them aright or you can leave them. Sometimes the crystals have their own agenda.

Starting with your center stone, touch it lightly and say, "Activate," Move out to one of the stones on the outside of the grid and touch it lightly and say, "Activate," then down to the next stone and say, "Activate," then back to the center stone touching that lightly and again repeating, "Activate".

You can follow this procedure all around your grid activating each stone and setting up the patterning,

You can also create a pattern depending on which grid shape you chose:  for the five pointed one you can activate the crystals doing the star pattern touching each point and then the center point. Or you can use the six-pointed star pattern by activating with two triangles and completing it with the center stone. The actual activation is up to you.

Your grid will remain active usually for 24 hours when you can re-activate it again. Or you can ask that it remain active for a week if you chose.

As soon as you finish your activation, you will or should feel this huge rush of energy and that will indicate that your grid is busy. So, go away and leave it alone and let it work.

If you do not feel this "rush" of energy, reactivate it one more time.

Sometimes it takes a few moments for the grid to configure energetically so go away and leave it alone. Don't worry. It is working on some level.

What if you don't feel any energy from your grid? If you followed all of the steps, then just leave it for 24 hours and let it do its work.

If your inner guidance is telling you that the grid just isn't working, stand by the grid and ask if you need to make some changes before you re-charge it again after 24 hours.

If you are being told that you need to make some changes, then carefully pick up one stone and ask if it is appropriate where it is in the grid. Depending on the answer, gently dismantle the grid giving thanks for the stones you did use. Then repeat the process using different stones.

Check the location, also, as that might be the answer, too.

When you feel that the grid is no longer needed, then dismantle it giving thanks to each stone and clearing them with running water and leaving them out in the sun for a few hours to recharge.

Here is something I wrote that might be helpful for working with crystals:

# Crystals and Your Aura:

Crystals are built from one of seven possible geometric forms: Triangle, squares, rectangles, hexagons, rhomboids, parallelograms, or trapeziums.

Three of these carry the distinct and easy to find sacred geometrical shapes, the triangle which is the tetrahedron (3 sides), the square (4 sides) which is the hexahedron and the hexagon (6 sides), which coincides with the icosahedron. The others, rectangles, rhomboids, parallelograms and trapeziums are all part of the square family either elongated or basically containing 4 sides. In Euclidean Plane Geometry, these are all considered quadrilateral polygons with 4 sides.  In my eyes, they are all from the hexahedron.

"Crystals are the Earth's DNA, a chemical imprint for evolution." so says Judy Hall in her book, The Crystal Bible, and "At the heart of each crystal is an atom and its component parts.  An atom is a dynamic, consisting of particles rotating around a center in constant motion.  So, although a crystal may look outwardly serene, it is actually a seething molecular mass vibrating at a certain frequency.  This is what gives a crystal its energy."

Almost like a little time bomb, each crystal is waiting to explode with the energy for which task (dedication) you have requested.

This rather changes the way you look at crystals, doesn't it?

When you hold a crystal in your hand, sometimes you will feel energy emanating from it, heat, vibration, cold, any of these sensations will let you know that this crystal that you are holding is a living, breathing object. Now you know that this crystal is sending out energetic vibrations into your electromagnetic shield.

"Whatever form they take, their crystalline structure can absorb, conserve, focus and emit energy, especially on the electromagnetic waveband." Judy Hall.

The Bio-magnetic Field or Sheath is the energy field that surrounds all living things, especially the human body. This Electromagnetic field is susceptible to electromagnetic wavebands or impulses. It will either accept or deflect these impulses. If the field is strong and protected, then the unwanted impulses will be bounced back to its source – most times in a transmuted and healing form.

Crystals that strengthen this Field, your Aura, will protect the inhabitant and deflect what is not for their best interests.  Most of you already know many of these crystals and have used them.  Just as a reminder, here are just a few:

<u>Amethyst clusters</u> will block geopathic stress when placed near your computer or in a room.

<u>Amethyst crystals</u> will cleanse the aura, heal holes, and draw in Divine Energy,

<u>Amber</u>, an ancient protector, draws off negative energy and cleans the aura,

<u>Apache Tear</u> gently protects the aura from absorbing negative energies,

<u>Citrine</u> cleanses and aligns the aura,

<u>Fluorite and Tourmaline</u> provide a psychic shield,

<u>Labradorite</u>, prevents energy leakage and aligns one to spiritual energies,

<u>Bloodstone</u>, an etheric cleanser,

<u>Magnetite</u> strengthens the aura,

<u>Clear Quartz</u>, cleanses, protects and increases the field sealing any holes,

<u>Selenite</u> detaches mental influences from the aura,

<u>Smokey Quartz</u>, grounds energy and dissolves negative patterns encased in the aura and absorbs negativity and electromagnetic smog.

<u>Tektite</u> strengthens the Bio-magnetic sheath around the body.    (One of my favorites)

One thing to remember when using your crystals, One or two programs for some intent will work wonders.  More than that will confuse the energies and probably negate what they were asked to do.  In this case more is NOT better.

Many years ago, when I was first introduced to crystals and their properties, and being an enthusiastic novice, I would wear crystals everywhere and carry bags of them around with me.  Now, I am much more selective.  The same holds true with crystal jewelry.  More is really not better.

Be selective, program them as needed and above all, keep them clean.  We wouldn't dream of venturing out each day without showering first and putting on clean clothes.  This also applies to your crystals.

May they be your constant companions, treat them as you would your old and dearest friends. They really are, you know.

# Part Three - Protecting Your Person

We have mentioned these areas before but included here are the crystals to protect you from them.

**Geopathic Stress**: –Stress that is created by subtle emanations and energy disturbances from underground water, power lines, and negative earth energy lines (ley lines). Geopathic stress runs through the earth and can affect and pollute people and buildings. It contributes to dis-ease of all kinds.

*Suggested crystals for protection are: Amazonite, Amethyst, Smoky Quartz, wear as appropriate.*

*Black Tourmaline can be worn but it is preferable to use it in an open grid to protect your home or room.*

**Electromagnetic smog or pollution:** -A subtle but detectable electromagnetic field that can have adverse effect on sensitive people. The smog is given off by electrical power lines, and items such as computers, cell phones, and televisions.

*Suggested crystals for protection are: Smokey Quartz, Lepidolite, Amazonite, Sodalite, wear or place as appropriate.*

**Sick Building Syndrome:** - The set of symptoms that accompany this syndrome are: headaches, dizziness, nausea, chest problems, and general fatigue. These symptoms sometimes indicate actual air pollution or inadequate ventilation, or negative environmental energies.

*Suggested Crystals for protection: Lepidolite, Sodalite, and Smokey Quartz. (Place around building or wear constantly.)*

**Entity Removal or Spirit Release:** - Detaching discarnate spirits or other beings and dispatching them to the appropriate post-death dimension.

*Suggested Crystals: Larimar, Amethyst, and Smokey Quartz. Wear on person for a short time until entity detaches.*

**Psychic Attack**: Malevolent thoughts or feelings toward another person, whether consciously or unconsciously directed, creating dis-ease and disruption in that person's life.

*Suggested Crystals to protect against psychic attack: Apache Tear, Rutilated Quartz, Selenite, Labradorite (wear constantly).*

*Black Tourmaline can be placed around room or building.*

**Psychic Vampirism**: The ability to draw off or 'feed off' the energy of others.

*Suggested Crystals for protection against Psychic Vampirism:*

*Green Aventurine, Fluorite, Iron Pyrite, Labradorite. Wear or carry constantly.*

*Black Tourmaline, Black Obsidian placed around room or building or carry in purse.*

NOTE:

Some people draw on other people's energies without realizing they are doing this. Examples would be a friend who is needy, or a co-worker who is going through a difficult time, or a client who is very negative.

Wearing a *Green Aventurine* on the spleen chakra will prevent other people from draining your energies. You can wear the stone in your bra underneath your left arm or tape one in place.

# Part Four - Protecting Your Home

Crystals will protect your home in several ways. They are decorative and pretty. Certain stones will enhance the energies within your home bring in prosperity and abundance (Citrine, carnelian and rose quart to name a few) and can keep your home harmonious and vibrant, a happy place to re-energize after a difficult day at work. Then there are other stones can repel negative energies, energies we inadvertently bring home with us.

Crystals will also protect your home from environmental pollution, or electronic smog caused by microwave ovens, cell phones, computers radio waves and radar radiation. They can also protect you from noisy, obnoxious neighbors.

Amethyst is a great protector stone, it brings in a very high spiritual vibration while guarding against psychic attack and ill wishing. It also blocks geopathic stress, environmental pollution and transmutes negativity.

An Amethyst cluster placed at your computer will deflect the negative emanations your computer sends.

Smokey Quartz acts like a vacuum cleaner, sucking up negativity replacing it with higher vibrations if the energy in your home has become polluted in any way.

If your home is near electrical power poles or a cell phone tower, Smokey Quartz placed on a windowsill near this device will deflect the bad away from your home.

If you have someone in your home that is putting out bad vibes or depressed energies, the Smokey Quartz will vacuum those energies away so as not to infect the entire house.

A Smokey Quartz crystal placed in your car or truck will protect both you and your passengers. Simply hold the crystal in your hand, visualize it surrounded with light and ask that it will give protection for your vehicle, your passengers and yourself.

Sodalite absorbs the emanations of high-frequency communication antennas, infrared microwaves, and radar. It also blocks out subtle emanations from your home computer. If your home has a lot of static, Sodalite will absorb it. You can make a Sodalite elixir and spray it around the room.

Inside Grids to protect your home.

Grid your house with Black Tourmaline by placing one in each corner beside the front door to block energies from entering. I use two on the floor and two above the door on the door frame. I also use a Black Tourmaline on each side of each of my windowsills.

I rarely place Black Tourmaline in a physical grid. I much prefer to use it around the house and know that I am protected that way.

NOTE: Always keep your black or dark stones separate from your other stones or crystals otherwise they can cancel out each other's energy

You can also place a Sodalite under each of the corners of your bed on the floor. Or between your mattress and box spring. Keeps out negative entities and ensures a good night's sleep.

# Part Five - Protecting Your Workplace

Crystals can be used in the workplace discreetly, (hidden in drawers, dropped along the edge of potted plants, or used as a paperweight – who's to know?). They can be used to enhance cooperation between co-workers or used to absorb electromagnetic smog. Line an amethyst up along the side of your computer and it will neutralize the effects of the computer's electromagnetic emanations.

<u>Green Aventurine</u> in the workplace will foster prosperity while it is busy promoting empathetic leadership, and at the same time, it will diffuse negative situations and turn them around. If you have a co-worker who leeches your energy, place one crystal in each drawer to shield you from energy drainage. (Or wear one under your left arm on the spleen chakra)

<u>Labradorite</u> enhances group energy and improves cooperation among co-workers. It encourages the acceptance of new ideas and the sharing of insights to benefit the whole, thus creating a harmonious working environment.

<u>Smokey Quartz</u> – our little vacuum cleaner sucks up any negative energy lurking around your space and protects you against other people's stress and frustration. It also alleviates communication difficulties. Keep one handy when Mercury goes retrograde.

<u>Sodalite</u> placed in the four corners of your room neutralizes the effect of sick building syndrome. Sodalite also absorbs emanations from fluorescent tubes and computers. This stone enhances the workings of a group, promoting companionship and harmony between co-workers.

Grids in the office might not be acceptable, so build your grid somewhere at home, place the name of your office and location on a slip of paper and place the information under the center stone. Grids work long distance, too.

# The Grids

# Personal Protection

There are times when you may feel the need to create a grid for yourself or for someone close to you that has shared problems or asked for your help.

NOTE: as with any spiritual work, you do need permission before you assist others.

To personalize a grid, you can write their name and location on a slip of paper and place it under the center stone. Or use a recent photo.

I touched briefly that grids can be used for long distance work and will go more in depth in the next book. For now, just know that grids are energy and you can send energy anywhere. Energy follows thought or intent.

WARNING: grids or any kind of energy work is only to be used for GOOD purposes, the Highest Good for all.

There is a Spiritual Law: The Law of Return. Whatever you send out returns to you. Some people call this Law, The Law of Attraction. Same Idea!

An easier way to set up a Personal Grid is to wear it!

A pendant and a stone in each pocket sets up a grid, a triangle.

Earrings and a pendant also creates a grid. The stones don't have to match, sometimes it is more powerful if the stones are mixed.

A single stone in your purse or backpack creates an enormous energy field around you. A clear crystal or an Amethyst does a remarkable job.

I carry a Smokey Quartz and a Labradorite in each pocket and have a Russian Lemurian Ice Quartz in my purse. (No wonder I never feel grounded.)

Jewelry is a wonderful way to protect yourself. There is a complete line of Tools of Evolution created by Paul Jensen who worked with Marcel Vogel earlier in his life. Paul created beautiful pendants incorporating Sacred Geometry. This is an easy way to 'wear your grids'.

A six-pointed grid is the Star of David.

This Star of David, a Tetrahedron, is Amethyst. My favorite most worn pendant.

You can purchase these pendants on www.exquisitecrystals.com

They are my only supplier.

The Five-Pointed Star is the Dodecahedron or the Pentagram.

This is a Columbian Obsidian Star of Venus. This Obsidian has most of the same qualities as Black Obsidian only it is easier to wear and not as 'strong'. I have one.

Beautiful, isn't it???

The Four-Pointed grid is the Hexahedron or the Earth Grid.

This Earth Heart is Golden Labradorite, highly protective stone. Wish I had one.

I do wear a Labradorite chip necklace.

Grids for personal protection

**Psychic attack:** concentrated and conscious malevolent thought and intent directed towards someone to bring about harm. Sometimes this is not consciously intended but done unconsciously as the person thinks negative thoughts about another person or discusses this person with someone else.

The grid I recommend is the Tektite Grid

**Entity Removal or Spirit Release:** - Detaching discarnate spirits or other beings and dispatching them to the appropriate post-death dimension.

*Suggested Crystals: Larimar, Amethyst, and Smokey Quartz. Wear on person for a short time until entity detaches.*

Amethyst Star of David.

**Psychic Vampirism**: The ability to draw off or 'feed off' the energy of others.

*Suggested Crystals for protection against Psychic Vampirism:*

*Green Aventurine, Fluorite, Iron Pyrite, Labradorite. Wear or carry constantly.*

*Black Tourmaline, Black Obsidian placed around room or building or carry in purse.*

Labradorite Earth Heart

# Protecting Your Home

**Geopathic Stress**: –Stress that is created by subtle emanations and energy disturbances from underground water, power lines, and negative earth energy lines (ley lines). Geopathic stress runs through the earth and can affect and pollute people and buildings. It contributes to dis-ease of all kinds.

*Suggested crystals for protection are: Amazonite, Amethyst, Smoky Quartz, wear as appropriate.*

A grid for this syndrome might be one with Amethyst Points.

**Electromagnetic smog or pollution:** -A subtle but detectable electromagnetic field that can have adverse effect on sensitive people. The smog is given off by electrical power lines, and items such as computers, cell phones, and televisions.

*Suggested crystals for protection are: Smokey Quartz, Lepidolite, Amazonite, Sodalite, wear or place as appropriate.*

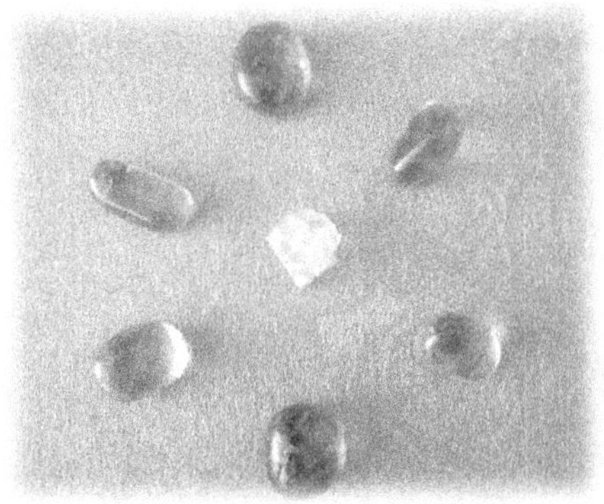

This grid is Smokey Quartz our little vacuum cleaner to suck up all that smog.

**Sick Building Syndrome:** - The set of symptoms that accompany this syndrome are: headaches, dizziness, nausea, chest problems, and general fatigue. These symptoms sometimes indicate actual air pollution or inadequate ventilation, or negative environmental energies.

*Suggested Crystals for protection: Lepidolite, Sodalite, and Smokey Quartz. (Place around building or wear constantly.)*

This grid has six Sodalites around an Apophyllite center stone.

Another way to grid your home is to get a copy of the layout of your house (Assessors Office) and set up a grid on the map.

# Protecting Your Workplace

Your grids for the Geopathic Stress, Electromagnetic Smog or pollution, and Sick Building Syndrome would work for your workplace, also. Any or all of these grids would be protection from any negativity around you and to keep your energy strong.

Green Aventurine polished stones in your desk drawers or in a potted plant would slip by un-noticed and increase everyone's prosperity. (Bonus!)

A paperweight f Labradorite might be interesting to some people.

Or an egg shaped polished Sodalite.

Although Sodalite would be much more effective if you could grid the room with a stone in each corner or grid the building the same way.

Or a dish filled with Smokey Quartz sitting on a windowsill would make a nice display.

Making a gem elixir is another way to clear spaces by using the elixir as a spritz or spray.

# Clearing Your Space

Need to clear a room but can't burn Sage?

I recommend a Smokeless Sacred Sage Spray for locations where you cannot use or burn Sage.

<u>Recipe</u>

Four-ounce bottle with cap and sprayer.

Organic Sacred Sage Essential Oil

Organic Lemongrass Essential Oil

Witch Hazel (pure)

Spring or distilled water

Fill a four-ounce bottle to about 2/3rds with spring or distilled water.

Add 1 tablespoon of Witch Hazel

Add 18 drops of Organic Sacred Sage Essential Oil

Add 18 drops of Organic Lemongrass Essential Oil

Cover tightly and shake well. Uncover and insert spray top. Spritz lightly to clear room.

Use this spray to clear spaces before doing any Spiritual or Energy work.

Have some entities hanging around and they just don't seem to want to leave? Try this.

Clearing Spaces Of Unwanted Energies.

You will need a set of four crystals (your choice), preferably with points.   and a drawing or map of the property to be cleared.

Place the map or drawing down on a clean and cleared space, using either a Smokeless spray, a Tibetan bowl, Reiki symbols, whatever you use to clear an area. Clear and center yourself before you begin. You can light a white candle and say a prayer.

"Guardians of the Light, I call upon you now, I ask you to clear this space and the entire property, remove any and all unwanted energies from the space and property and sweep them away, send them back to where they originated and ask that they be transmuted back into unconditional love and light." (This will include any and all energies hanging out there.)

Next: place your crystals on each corner of the map or drawing (four crystals, four corners)

Point the crystals out from the house and the property and link them together by touching each one and asking it to seal and protect you and all the family members who reside on the property.

Next,

Ask the Creator of the Light to fill and surround the property and all members residing within to be filled and surrounded with the Pure White Light. Ask that they be filled and surrounded with this Divine Pure White Light and that they be protected.

Now, see the property and each family member surrounded and filled with this Divine Pure White Light and ask that the property and all residing therein be protected now and forevermore.

Bow and say thank you to all of the beings there that made this possible.

Walk away from the grid and know and believe that the Angels will handle the rest.

That should do it.

That ends this book. Stay tuned for the next book in the series:

Crystal Grids for Healing coming in 2019.

Here are the links for my other Crystal books.

Other Crystal Books by S. D. Anderson, Ph.D. available on Amazon.com

*Creating Crystal Grids for Beginners*

A step by step guide to creating your grids.

https://www.amazon.com/Creating-Crystal-Grids-Sharon-Anderson-ebook/dp/B00BPCWKI2/

*Sacred Grids*

A guide to using the Sacred Geometry connection in grids

https://www.amazon.com/Sacred-Grids-Creating-Crystal-Geometry-ebook/dp/B00UDMZN4S/

*Crystal Grids: Activating the 12 Strands of DNA*

An advanced book on grids

https://www.amazon.com/Crystal-Grids-Activating-Strands-DNA-ebook/dp/B0182I7L1M/

# About the Author

Sharon D. Anderson, PhD, RMT

Sharon is an Author/Publisher, dedicated to her craft for more than 30 years. Writing in her genre, Visionary Fiction and Non-Fiction, all of her books, websites and blogs merge a far-seeing perspective of New Age and Ancient Wisdom from Eastern and Western Philosophies.

She is a member of both the Cape Cod Writer's Center and the Visionary Fiction Alliance. She recently founded the Cape Cod Writer's Studio which meets weekly in Dennisport, where she teaches members how to self-publish their work, supporting them on their paths to publication in the digital world.

Here is the link to her Amazon Authors Page:

https://www.amazon.com/author/andersonsharon

Her Good Reads Author Page:

https://www.goodreads.com/angelicomm

E-mail: sdanderson.books@gmail.com

Her Blog  https://www.audacious-author.com

Her website:

https://www.audacious-publisher.com

Are you a writer? Would you like free information about self-publishing?

Become a member of the Cape Cod Writer's Studio. All you need is your e-mail address. I promise you we DO NOT e-mail you constantly. You may even think we may have forgotten you.

Go to

www.audacious-publisher.com

Look under the Cape Cod Writer's Studio page, click there for the drop-down menu and see the member signup link. After you sign up, I am supposed to remember to send you a free gift. If I forget, shoot me (?) an e-mail to remind me.

I know there is an easier way, but I haven't figured that out yet.

Thanks so much

I do write other silly books. Here is the series I was working on until this book was screaming so loud, I had to put *Something Witchy This Way Comes* on hold.

Here is an excerpt:

# SOMETHING WITCHY

*This way comes...*

*by*

*S. D. Anderson*

*"By the pricking of my thumbs,*

*Something Wicked this way comes."*

Macbeth, Act IV, Scene I

by William Shakespeare

Macbeth, Act I, Scene I

Thunder and Lightning.

Enter three Witches.

FIRST WITCH – (Wendy)

When shall we three meet again?

In thunder, lightning, or in rain?

SECOND WITCH – (Willa)

When the hurly-burly's done,

When the battle's lost and won.

THIRD WITCH – (Waldo, her dad wanted a boy)

That will be ere the set of sun.

FIRST WITCH – (Wendy)

Where the place?

SECOND WITCH – (Willa)

Upon the heath.

THIRD WITCH – (Waldo)

There to meet with Macbeth.

FIRST WITCH – (Wendy)

I come, Graymalkin (her gray cat)

SECOND WITCH – (Willa)

Paddock calls. (a toad)

THIRD WITCH – (Waldo)

Anon. (see you soon)

ALL

Fair is foul, and foul is fair;

Hover through the fog and filthy air.

They exit.

Planet Earth

A Witch's Wake

One Rainy Afternoon

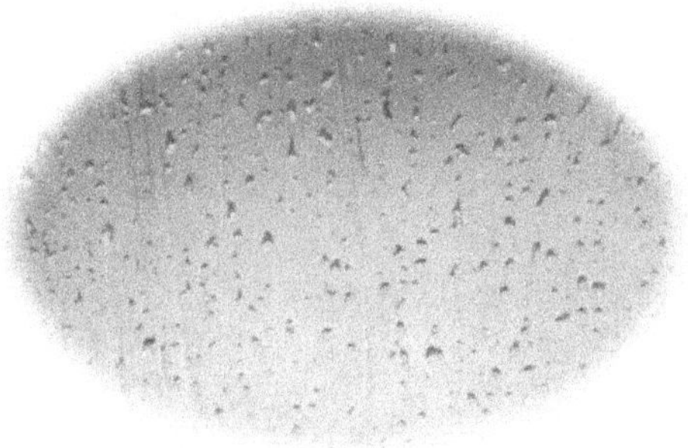

Chapter One

"My poor Gwendolyn," sobbed Glynnis Gwittmore, Goodwitch of the South, as she wrung out her black lace edged hankie for the third time, "she was always doing spells to help other witches, I will miss her, and her wandering wart."

The sad, bereft mourners assembled around the casket were still stunned by the suddenness of the death of their dearly departed witch. Dressed appropriately as all traditional witches did; black pointy boots, black stockings, long black dresses, tall pointy hats, only today out of respect to the deceased, they wore long black veils hiding their tears, which they dabbed delicately with black lace trimmed hankies.

"To have a house fall on her was cruel, especially during a tornado. My poor Gwendolyn was merely conjuring a few spells standing on that hillside. She had done that countless times before, using the lightening to enhance her spells. How was she to know that a tornado was coming up the hill just as she howled the last incantation? How was she to know that a house was inside that funnel ready to fall down to earth? Blindsided! Bashed! My poor Gwendolyn Gwittmore, Good Witch of the East. She shall be sadly, sadly, missed," eulogized Glynnis to those around her.

She was devastated. She was about to be even more devastated as the will was being read, which was not usually done before poor deceased (Gwendolyn) was put in the ground. It seems there was a glitch. The solicitor was very uncomfortable as he read the clause in this particular will that stated: there was no place for witches to go in Heaven.

"You must be mistaken!" Glynnis choked through her weeping, as she rung out her previous tears from the already saturated hankie. "My sister was an exemplary witch. She was always kind and compassionate, continually thinking of others." She dissolved into another round of tears. The solicitor, a kindly old man, opened one of the desk drawers, pulled out a box of tissues and handed it to her.

"No, my dear, I am deadly serious, (pardon the pun), according to our records and our research, Witches cannot go to Heaven because there is no final destination for them, no place for them to stay." Mr. Bentley-Smythe sadly replied.

"What are we to do?" Glynnis asked tearfully, "we can't just leave her where she is. What do you recommend?"

"Unfortunately, there is nothing I can think of. There is, however, another clause in this will. She did leave you some property, a rather large holding but not worth anything in today's market."

"She did? I was not aware that she had any property."

"It was left to you both by your great, great, great, great grandmother, and upon either of your deaths, it was to pass to the next of kin."

"Where is this property? She never mentioned it to me."

"It is somewhere in the Petrified Forest. I have the exact coordinates in another document in the office safe."

"Does anyone live there? Are there any tenants?"

"I hardly think so. The forest is fossilized." Mr. Bentley-Smythe replied, "no one could live there. It is uninhabitable."

"Oh, that seems to be another dead end," Glynnis replied sadly, tears threatening again. Then, as if a ray of sunshine pushed itself through the gray clouds, an idea began to form. She sat up straight in her chair and a huge smile lit her face. "but, it could be the solution."

"I'm sorry, my dear, I'm not following you," Mr. Bentley-Smythe replied, "how could that possibly be the solution?"

"If it is not habitable for anyone here on Earth, could it possibly be a place for witches to live when they go to Heaven?"

Mr. Bentley-Smythe thought and thought.

"Well, could they?" she asked again, almost dancing with impatience.

"Well, my dear, I have no idea, but, it is certainly worth a try."

"So, how would we do this?" she asked anxiously now that a solution was in sight.

"You could 'bequeath' the land to Heaven. That sort of transaction is done all the time." Mr. Bentley-Smythe assured her, "well, almost all the time," wondering how that would work.

"Good, then let's do that." She wiped her eyes, blew her nose, and felt hopeful for the first time since the dreadful accident had happened. "Let's go on with the funeral, my sister deserves a decent burial. What happens to her after that Only Heaven Knows."